MASTERING
PHYSICS

Understanding the Laws of Motion

KRISTEN PETERSEN

Cavendish Square
New York

Published in 2015 by Cavendish Square Publishing, LLC
243 5th Avenue, Suite 136, New York, NY 10016

CPSIA Compliance Information: Batch #WW15CSQ

All websites were available and accurate when this book was sent to press.

Library of Congress Cataloging-in-Publication Data

Petersen, Kristen.
Understanding the laws of motion / by Kristen Petersen.
p. cm. — (Mastering physics)
Includes index.
ISBN 978-1-50260-140-7 (hardcover) ISBN 978-1-50260-136-0 (ebook)
1. Motion — Juvenile literature. I. Title.
QC133.5 P484 2015
531—d23

Editor: Fletcher Doyle
Senior Copy Editor: Wendy A. Reynolds
Art Director: Jeffrey Talbot
Senior Graphic Designer: Amy Greenan
Senior Production Manager: Jennifer Ryder-Talbot
Production Editor: David McNamara
Photo Research by J8 Media

The photographs in this book are used by permission and through the courtesy of: Cover photo and page 1, Danleo/
File:Leaving Yongsan Station.jpg; flickr.com/photos/brenda_starr/2984808217/Wikimedia Commons; dennisvdw/
iStock/Thinkstock, 5; Sergiy Serdyuk/iStock/Thinkstock, 6; Amy Greenan, 8; Amy Greenan, 9; SCIEPRO/Science
Photo Library/Getty Images, 10; Marco Govel/Shutterstock,12; Leon Halip/Getty Images Sport/Getty Images, 15;
ESO/File:ESO/Halley 1986 by ESO gpo 1386002-cc.jpg/Wikimedia Commons, 16; baku13/105mm tank gun
Rifling.jpg/Wikimedia Commons, 19; Fuse/Thinkstock, 20; Tom Shaw/Getty Images Sport/Getty Images, 23; Print
Collector/Hulton Archive/ Getty Images, 25; Hemera Technologies/AbleStock.com/Thinkstock, 27; ChrisWPhoto/
Shutterstock, 28; David McNew/Getty Images News/Getty Images 30; Keystone/Hulton Archive/ Getty Images,
32; Rudi Von Briel/Photolibrary/Getty Images, 34; Multi-bits/The Image Bank/Getty Images, 37; Airwolf/File:Türk
Yıldızları 2210.JPG/ Wikimedia Commons, 38; Ker Robertson/Getty Images Sport/Getty Images, 40; Amy
Greenan, 41; Amy Greenan, 42.

Printed in the United States of America

CONTENTS

INTRODUCTION

I f you drive your car too fast as you turn a corner, the results are as predictable as the increase in the cost of your auto insurance. Your car will not be able to change direction quickly enough, and you will go off the road.

When engineers design roads, they determine maximum speeds on curves using mathematical formulas. To do this, they use information such as the motion and direction of a car in the curve, the mass of the car, and the forces acting on that car.

Sir Isaac Newton (1642–1727) discovered the concept that any motion can be explained mathematically. He developed a new kind of math for making calculations on problems with changing variables, such as a car changing direction. It is called calculus.

Newton worked out a single system for describing how the universe works. He formulated the law of universal gravitation, which applies even in space, and the three laws of motion.

Newton's laws belong to classical physics, which apply to all things with two exceptions: those traveling at or near the speed of light, and those at the atomic level. The electrons, protons, and other matter that make up the atom are governed by rules of their own. These fall under the realm of quantum physics.

The laws of motion are the building blocks of the science of physics, which is the study of forces, energy, and matter. Classical or Newtonian physics is concerned with the way in which matter responds to **forces**, as well as the way in which forces act on matter. Since all matter is subject to forces, everything on the planet (living and nonliving) is subject to the laws of physics. Some of the

Several laws of physics govern the flight of a snowboarder.

most basic laws in physics are about motion. These laws were not invented—they were discovered through observation.

Physics can be applied to anything you do, whether it's riding a skateboard, shooting a basketball, or moving your bedroom furniture. Understanding these laws can also help you design more fuel-efficient cars that are better for the environment, construct a ramp to improve wheelchair access to your home or a public building, or build a better snowboard. Classical physics describes an ideal world through these laws.

Jet engines provide the force for the acceleration needed for takeoff.

ONE

What Is Motion?

Anyone who has ever watched a four-year-old knows they are constantly in motion while they're awake. However, they have nothing on the Earth, because it never sleeps. Everything on our planet is constantly in motion because the Earth is spinning and orbiting the sun. Motion is an action that occurs when something moves from point *A* to point *B*. We measure the motion of objects in relation to their surroundings.

In studying motion and the forces that act on motion, the most important factors to determine are **magnitude** (size), direction, **speed** (the rate of movement), **velocity**, and displacement (the distance moved from the starting point to the end point). Magnitude, direction, speed, velocity, and displacement are expressed mathematically with numbers and formulas.

These mathematical quantities are divided into two categories: **scalars** and **vectors**. Scalars describe a magnitude only. Time and distance are scalars. For example, one hour and five miles are both scalar quantities.

Vectors describe both magnitude and direction. Direction is as important in the study of motion as magnitude is. Knowing that

Jose's Deli is five miles away does not help anyone find it. However, if the person looking for the store knows that it is five miles north, south, east, or west of a certain landmark, that helps a great deal. It is necessary to know the direction an object has traveled to calculate its displacement, or how far it has traveled.

Speed is a measure of how fast an object is moving without regard to its direction. It is a scalar quantity. Speed is always measured in terms of time—how fast an object is going within a certain time frame—per hour, per minute, or per second.

Velocity measures the rate at which an object changes its position. It is a vector quantity because it concerns both magnitude and direction.

NASCAR drivers, for example, can hit speeds of 200 miles per hour (320 kilometers per hour) but have a velocity of zero after a trip around the track because they end up where they started. Or, let's say a person taking sixteen minutes to get to Jose's Deli has a velocity of 30 miles per hour (48 kmh). After returning with their food, their velocity returns to zero, no matter how long the trip took.

A vector diagram is an illustration of an object while it is moving. It shows direction and magnitude.

CHANGING SPEEDS

Acceleration changes motion so that it is no longer uniform. Acceleration is not the same as either speed or velocity. While speed measures the rate of motion, and velocity measures rate of motion and its direction, acceleration measures how quickly velocity changes. Acceleration is a vector quantity because it has both magnitude and direction.

In physics, acceleration includes slowing down as well as speeding up. An object with a constant (uniform) velocity is not accelerating because it is neither slowing down nor speeding up. In order to calculate acceleration, or the rate of change of motion, it is necessary to understand the vectors involved. The rate of change in the motion of an object depends on time, speed, and direction. An object at rest has zero motion, zero acceleration, and zero velocity or speed. When it begins to move, it accelerates. It will continue to move at a steady rate unless another force is applied to increase its velocity, decrease its velocity, or stop it altogether.

A car driving at 35 miles per hour (56 kmh) may change its speed to 50 miles per hour (80 kmh) or to 20 miles per hour (32 kmh). Either way, it is technically accelerating—although for clarity, we usually say that speeding up is accelerating and slowing down is decelerating.

Acceleration may be constant, or increase in definite units, from one to two to three to four for a period of time until the acceleration levels off or stops. The rate of acceleration may change second by second: faster, slower, faster, slower. Acceleration is always limited by natural forces—gravity, **friction**, or **tension**.

DISTANCE VERSUS DESTINATION

Distance is a scalar quantity that measures how much ground a moving object covers during its motion. It is expressed in linear measurements—centimeters, inches, miles, kilometers, and so forth. On the other hand, displacement is a vector quantity measuring how far the moving object has traveled from its origin. It describes the object's change in position from a starting point.

Think of it in terms of a right triangle. For example, let's say a car travels four miles east, then turns north and travels three miles.

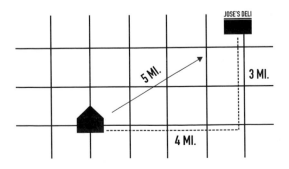

It will have driven a distance of seven miles, but its displacement is five miles because that is the linear distance from its starting point.

What Is Uniform Motion?

When someone puts their car on cruise control, they are trying to get it to maintain a steady, unchanging speed. This is usually done to avoid a speeding ticket, but what is achieved is actually a kind of **uniform motion**. In our world, it is very difficult to maintain uniform motion because of friction and gravity. Usually objects accelerate, which means to speed up or

The forces that affect the orbits of the planets are unchanging and in balance.

slow down. The speed of a car on cruise control can be changed by wind, hills, and braking to avoid other drivers.

Planets in orbit maintain uniform motion because the forces that act on them and keep them in motion are balanced. This means that the gravitational pull of the sun on the planets is balanced by the speed or forward motion of the planets. If they were to become unbalanced, a planet would either plunge into the sun or fly in a straight line out of orbit. Although objects in motion want to move in a straight line, a planet is held in orbit by the constant gravitational attraction of the sun. Astronomers can predict exactly where the planets will be on any given date because of this.

Constant, or uniform, speed can be determined simply by dividing the distance covered by the time taken to travel that distance. The formula is $r = d / t$, or: the rate of speed is equal to distance traveled, divided by the time it takes to travel that distance. When the speedometer in a car reads 35 miles per hour (56 kmh), it means that it takes one hour for that car at that speed to travel 35 miles (56 km). The distance, 35 miles (56 km), is divided by the time, one hour, to give a rate of 35 miles per hour (56 kmh).

TWO

Making Things Go

I f you need to get your car fixed, you call a mechanic who knows about machines and how they work. In physics, however, the term mechanics has a different definition, instead referring to the motion of objects as well as the forces and energies that act upon these objects in motion.

Mechanics is divided into two parts: **kinematics** and **dynamics**. Kinematics deals with how objects move, without regard to the cause of the motion. Objects may move in a straight line or take a circular path. Dynamics deals with forces and energy to explain why objects move as they do. The force behind a motion may be applied, such as steam, or it may be constant, such as the pull of gravity.

Motion is dimensional because it takes up space (dimension) and requires time. The dimension of time (t) is always implied in motion because a change in location takes time to accomplish. Without time, there is no movement, just as there is no movement without direction.

The dimensions of motion are the direction that motion takes. In real life, motion has many dimensions because objects may go in many directions. Determining the direction of motion is the first step in understanding the mechanics of motion. For example, in a hockey game, pucks follow the basic form of motion, which is linear.

Linear motion is movement in a straight line. All motion begins as linear. If a force prevents it from moving forward in a straight line, it angles off, as a hockey puck does when it hits a skate, stick, or goal post. Any object that is heavier than air and is dropped falls in a linear motion.

When an object is propelled or expelled by force it becomes a projectile—and the only force acting upon it is gravity. Projectiles travel in a **trajectory**, or a curved path, through space. They may be thrown or propelled vertically (upward or downward) or horizontally.

A thrown baseball or football is a projectile. Because of the pull of gravity, once the ball leaves the player's hand, it has a constant downward acceleration. A football often is thrown with an arc, but the pull of gravity slows the ball's original upward speed and then increases its downward speed as it falls back to Earth.

A baseball pitcher snaps or rotates his wrist, which puts spin on the ball to make it move as it approaches the plate. Air moves faster in the direction of the ball's spin, creating lower air density and less pressure on the side of the ball than on the front of the ball. This causes the ball to move in the direction of the spin. This movement is called the Magnus effect. Named for German physicist Gustav Magnus, this movement also explains why a soccer ball "bends" after it spins off the instep of a player, or how a fastball in baseball seems to defy gravity and rise as it approaches the plate.

In baseball, the ball is always thrown with a downward trajectory, since the pitcher is on a mound and the batter on flat ground. Since no major league pitcher, even one able to throw a ball 100 miles per hour (62 kmh), is capable of throwing a ball with nearly enough force to overcome gravity, a fastball can never really rise. Instead, it can be thrown with backspin, creating an upward force on the ball that reduces downward acceleration. This causes the fastball to drop less quickly than other pitches, giving it the illusion of rising.

A pitcher uses spin to alter the flight of the ball.

GOING IN CIRCLES

If an object is moving at a constant speed, but for some reason cannot move in a straight line, it will travel in a circle to keep moving.

Planets have elliptical orbits so they are not always the same distance from the sun. However, these distances are relatively small, so their orbits are practically circular. The planets are prevented from continuing out into space in a straight line because gravity pulls them back toward the sun. They are locked into their orbits by their speed and the force of gravity.

Comets, which have truly elliptical orbits, are another story. They are in orbit in our solar system, but the forces of gravity on

The return of Halley's Comet turned out to be predictable.

Understanding the Laws *of* Motion

them change as they speed by planets. Halley's Comet is named for English astronomer Edmond Halley and is the best known of the comets. Halley calculated in 1705 that the comets seen in 1531, 1607, and 1682 were one and the same, and predicted that it would return in 1758. It did.

Halley's Comet returns every seventy-six years on average, but changing gravitational forces have altered its orbit enough to vary the rate of its appearances by a year or two.

Centripetal force keeps pulling a rotating object toward the center of what it's rotating around so that it doesn't fly away. There appears to be a force pulling it away from the center as well. This is called centrifugal force, but instead of being a real force, it is really the object's tendency toward linear motion, away from the center of a circle.

If an object turns around an axis (a straight line or pole), it is demonstrating rotary motion. A spinning bicycle wheel is an example of rotary motion. All spinning objects will continue to rotate in a circle until gravity or friction slows them down. At this point they will need applied energy. This means that unless you are going downhill, the friction of your bike tires will slow you down—so keep pedaling.

Ballistics Report

In many television shows, crimes are solved through the use of ballistics—the science of the motion of projectiles. There are three types of ballistics: interior ballistics examines how the projectile reacts inside the barrel; exterior ballistics examines how the projectile flies; and terminal ballistics examines what the effect of the projectile will be on its target.

Internal ballistics experts in crime labs study what happens to a bullet from the moment the trigger is pulled (ignition) until it exits the gun barrel. With the exception of shotguns and rocket launchers, firearms have spiral grooves, called rifling, inside their barrels. These distinct grooves cause the bullet to spin, which creates stability as it flies toward its target. For every rifle or pistol, the depth, diameter, and number of turns in the rifling vary. Fins and feathers provide this stability in rockets and arrows. If an arrow or a model rocket begin to tumble (end over end), the fins provide drag at the bottom of the projectile, which pushes the bottom back under the nose of the projectile in the direction of the flight path.

When a bullet is fired, its metal scrapes against the gun's grooves. Irregularities inside the gun barrel leave tiny markings on the bullet, creating a distinct "fingerprint." These markings allow ballistics experts to match a bullet to the gun that fired it.

All projectiles that have been fired are subject to gravity, air resistance, wind, and drift. Long-range cannon or rockets also need to account for the Earth's rotation; if projectiles are in the air long enough their target will move. Exterior ballistics experts will account for all of these things to ensure projectiles reach their targets. For example, they calibrate the angle at which a bullet must be fired at a distant target to counter the effect of gravity, which starts the moment the bullet leaves the barrel.

Terminal ballistics solves problems such as what speed a shell must have to penetrate a tank's armor. It helps scientists develop better weapons and stronger defenses.

The spin the rifling of a gun barrel imparts provides in-flight stability to the bullet, which otherwise would tumble.

The driver will impart force to this golf ball so it will not stay at rest.

THREE

Newton's Giant Step Forward

S ir Isaac Newton (1642–1727) famously said, "If I have seen further, it is by standing on the shoulders of giants." In this way he acknowledged the contribution of those who came before him to our understanding of our world.

In science, no one stands taller than Newton. Through studying gravity, he determined that the same results always happen under the same circumstances, and formulated three laws to explain what he observed about motion. These three laws predict what will happen when an object starts to move or stops moving, and they explain why this happens. They are the basis of mechanics, the science of motion.

His first law is that an object at rest tends to stay at rest and an object in motion tends to stay in motion with the same speed and in the same direction unless acted upon by another force. Or, any object not subject to outside forces remains at a constant velocity (even if the velocity is zero) covering equal distances in equal times along a straight-line path.

INERTIA

Newton's first law is often called the law of **inertia**, which is an object's tendency to resist acceleration. It states that if an object is not being pushed or pulled by a force, it will either stay still or keep moving at a steady speed.

Before Newton, people thought that moving objects would eventually stop moving on their own. Newton proved that objects slow down, speed up, or stop moving only when a force outside themselves makes them.

Resistance to slowing down is called **momentum**. Momentum is the tendency of an object to continue moving, whether it moves at a steady rate or accelerates. Momentum has both magnitude (size) and direction. It is a vector quantity. The mathematical quantity for momentum (p) can be found by multiplying **mass** (m) times velocity (v).

$$p = m \times v$$

This measures the constant or unchanging movement of a moving object, whereas acceleration measures the changing rate of a moving object.

Momentum can be changed only by changing the object's velocity through acceleration or by changing its mass.

Similar to inertia is equilibrium, the state in which all forces are perfectly balanced—there is just as much pull as push. In a state of equilibrium, it takes the presence of a new force to trigger acceleration. This new force causes the balanced system to be unbalanced and brings about acceleration. Newton's second law explains this concept.

GETTING THINGS MOVING

Newton's second law states that the acceleration of an object as produced by a net force is directly proportional to the magnitude of the net force, in the same direction as the net force, and inversely proportional to the mass of the object. This can be represented

The mass of the ship gives it a decided edge in momentum over the unfortunate sailboat in this collision in the United Kingdom.

mathematically by $a = Fm$, although the equation is normally written as $F = ma$, where F is force, m is mass, and a is acceleration.

More simply put, when a force acts on an object, the object accelerates in the direction the force is pushing or pulling it. If you push something forward, it goes forward. The greater the object's mass, the more force is needed to make it move.

A proportional effect directly impacts the object. For instance, doubling the force that is used on an object will make the object accelerate twice as fast. An inverse proportional effect has an opposite impact on an object. If a constant force is applied, doubling the mass will make the object's acceleration one-half as large. Newton's second law emphasizes the concept of mass. Mass is the amount of matter an object has. Every object has mass, but some objects are denser than others because their matter is more

Change of Method

S ir Isaac Newton is best known for his three laws of motion and his study of gravity, but he also made a great contribution to science by outlining a way of exploring the natural world while removing any bias from our investigations.

In his 1687 book *Mathematical Principles of Natural Philosophy*, he spelled out four rules for scientific reasoning. These are: assign only those causes to natural things that are true and sufficient to explain them; the same natural effects must be assigned to the same causes; if two or more bodies are the same, they must share the same qualities; and things deduced from observation of phenomena should be viewed as accurate until contradicted by other phenomena.

His work built on the advances made by others. The most important advances were made by Galileo (1564–1642). Galileo demonstrated the benefits of experimentation over philosophical approaches for explaining why things happen, and showed that physics should be mathematics based.

In this way, Newton formalized the scientific method we use today. Here's one variation.

1. Make observations and raise a question.
2. Gather data through research that might answer the question.
3. Propose a hypothesis.
4. Design and perform an experiment to test the hypothesis.
5. Analyze your test results to draw conclusions.

Sir Isaac Newton designed an experiment to observe what happens to light when it is shined through a prism.

compact. Size is important in determining mass, but density is more important. Air is not very dense, but metal is, so a ball bearing has more mass than a balloon, although a balloon may be much larger.

Mass influences the motion of an object. Given a constant force, the greater the object's mass, the slower it can change its velocity. Mass is significant not just because it describes how large and heavy an object is, but also because it is the measure of an object's inertia. The more mass an object has, the more inertia it has. For example, a box filled with bricks has more inertia than an equal-size box filled with Styrofoam, and it will take more force to move it. The box with less resistance to movement has less mass.

Newton's third law states that the force that is exerted on one body by a second body is equal in magnitude and opposite in direction to the force exerted by the second body on the first. Or, if an object is pushed or pulled, it will push or pull to an equal extent in the opposite direction. This is often restated as, "For every action, there is an equal and opposite reaction."

Whenever object A and object B interact with each other, they exert forces upon one another. If a man pushes on a heavy van, he will feel the van push back on him. When a girl on ice skates pushes against the wall that runs along the rink, she will slide back on the ice. The direction of the force on the first object is opposite to the direction of the force on the second object.

When you step into a boat, you exert a force that moves it from the pier. You should step quickly, and don't keep one foot on the pier—otherwise, you will be going for a swim.

NOTHING'S LOST

The law of conservation of momentum is an offshoot of Newton's third law and is a fundamental concept of classical physics. It states that the total momentum of all bodies in a closed system is constant and not affected by processes occurring within the system. A closed system is one that doesn't allow an exchange of matter from outside the system and isn't subject to any force from outside the system. The "processes occurring within the system" usually refers to a collision between objects.

There is no momentum lost when the cue ball strikes other balls in billiards.

Conservation of momentum governs the game of billiards. The object of the game is to make the cue ball collide with another ball so that the second ball will move in a specific direction. The collisions may be straight-on or off-center, and the skilled player will know exactly where to aim the cue ball and how hard to send it to get the desired result. The momentum of the cue ball is transferred to the ball it hits, which gives it enough momentum to travel into a pocket. In a collision, the momentum lost by one object is gained by the object it hits. The total amount of momentum remains constant. What object A loses is gained by object B.

The law of conservation of momentum is expressed mathematically as $mv_1 = mv_2$, where m is mass and v is velocity. The forces are equal in magnitude, but they are opposite in direction. The total momentum of two objects before a collision is equal to the total momentum of the two objects after the collision.

Conservation of momentum occurs in the collision of a baseball bat with a pitched ball. When a batter hits a baseball, the momentum of the bat just before it strikes the ball plus the momentum of the pitched baseball is equal to the momentum of the bat after it strikes the ball plus the momentum of the hit baseball. However, the mass of the bat is greater than the mass of the ball, so it exerts greater force—and the ball will experience greater acceleration.

Newton's Giant Step Forward

The weight of the bouncing child creates an interaction between the trampoline and the shoes.

FOUR

Changing Motion

Newton's laws of motion have many complex applications, but they can be stated easily. Newton's first law states that an object will remain at rest or in motion unless some force, acting upon that object, will change its state, causing the object to start moving, accelerate, change its direction, or bring it to a stop. If an object is already in motion, no force is needed to keep it moving, as inertia will accomplish that.

If a force acts on an object at rest and there is no opposing force, it will accelerate in the direction of the force. This is Newton's second law.

Force exists when there is an interaction between two objects; that is, when one object pushes or pulls the other. This is Newton's third law. For example, a tow truck applies force to pull a car that can't start, or a tugboat applies force to push a barge into port. Some forces are not so obvious, however. Magnetic fields may attract or repel an object only slightly. Gravity is such a common pull that we are hardly aware of it. Obvious or not, when the interaction stops, the objects no longer experience force.

Force is measured in newtons. One newton is the amount of force required to give a 1-kilogram mass an acceleration of 1 meter/(second × second) ($1m/s^2$). A newton is abbreviated as N. Ten newtons of force is written as 10 N.

Forces can be divided into two categories: forces that touch the object and forces that work from a distance and are not in contact with the object. Gravity and electromagnetism work from a distance. Friction and tension work by contact.

Understanding the Laws *of* Motion

Tugboats apply force to barges and other large ships when they are in a harbor.

GRAVITATIONAL PULL

Gravity is the pull of one object toward the center of the mass of another. On Earth, we usually think of gravity as pulling downward. In space, the force of one body, such as Earth, the moon, or another massively large object, attracts other objects toward itself. The force gravity exerts on an object is exactly proportional to the object's mass. This means that the more massive an object is, the greater the pull of gravity will be.

Gravity of the Situation

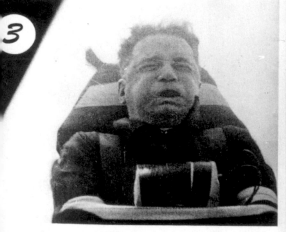

The effects of high levels of g-force are evident on the face of John Stapp in 1954.

The advent of the airplane and its use as a weapon in World War I exposed man to something rarely felt before: gravity forces. As these planes became faster and more maneuverable they became more dangerous because they increased gravity forces on pilots. The result was that pilots were losing consciousness during dogfights, or air battles at short range marked by quick changes in direction.

Normal gravity on Earth is given a value of one and any number given to gravity forces is a multiple of normal gravity. At 5 g's, a person experiences a force equal to five times his or her weight. Gravity forces have more to do with acceleration–the change in speed over time–than with speed itself. How much gravity force can man withstand?

A CART driver at Texas Motor Speedway experiences 5 g's of force in the turns. That can take its toll on a body when felt over the course of a race, but humans can survive much more for short periods. John Stapp, an Air Force physician, tried to find out how much he could withstand. In his last experiment, in December 1954, he used nine solid-fuel rockets on a sled to accelerate to 632 miles per hour (1,017 kmh) in five seconds, and then came to a dead stop in just over one second. He experienced 46.2 g's and lived.

More harmful to humans than the magnitude of the g-force is the direction of the force. We can deal with horizontal forces, front to back or side to side, much more easily than vertical forces, or up and down. This is because of blood pressure. In normal gravity, we need 22 millimeters of mercury blood pressure to get blood from our hearts to our brains. At 2 g's, we need twice the blood pressure. When the g-forces hit three or more of head-to-toe pressure, blood pools in our lower extremities, our brains don't get enough oxygen, and we pass out.

Fighter pilots today counter g-forces by using suits that use air bladders to squeeze the stomach and lower extremities to keep blood in their upper bodies. This gives them the ability to withstand up to 9 g's.

We use g-force to measure acceleration due to gravity. The normal, earthbound "g" is 1. We can feel the results of anything less or more in our bodies. NASA (National Aeronautics and Space Administration) has studied the effects of weightlessness (0 g) for years and has developed ways to lessen its detrimental effects. Among these effects are loss of muscle mass—muscles relax because they aren't needed to resist gravity—and loss of bone density, which leaves astronauts susceptible to breaking them. Astronauts exercise to counter these detrimental effects in space, but they still need months to rehabilitate after a long mission.

Under natural conditions, there is no situation that involves long-term weightlessness on Earth. However, it is possible for a person to feel weightless for a second or two if he or she is thrown up into the air by mechanical means.

Water on a highway reduces friction between a car's tires and the road.

Understanding the Laws *of* Motion

A REAL DRAG

The most common force that causes objects to slow down (accelerate in a negative direction) is friction. Friction acts as a drag on an object's speed. It is a force applied in the opposite direction of an object's velocity.

All objects, including liquids, solids, and gases provide friction. The friction in sandpaper quickly wears away a surface. Highways are built to provide the right amount of friction for tires. Too little friction (bald tires or icy conditions) can be hazardous because the car will not be able to stay on the road and will slide off. Friction is necessary for slowing or stopping a vehicle.

Air resistance is a frictional force that acts upon objects as they travel through air. It opposes the motion of the object. Downhill skiers position their bodies to reduce air resistance. Race cars are designed to encounter as little air resistance as possible.

Objects traveling through water also meet resistance. Think about how much more effort, or force, you need to use to move through water than to move through air.

Friction can be overcome by applying lubrication or smoothing a surface. Moving heavy furniture on a rug requires a lot of force because the rug creates a lot of friction. Putting a slider under the legs of the furniture smoothes the surface, reducing friction, so it takes less effort to push the object.

TYPES OF FORCE

There are other forces that act upon objects, including applied force, **normal force,** spring force, and tensional force.

Applied force is a force applied to an object by a person or another object. It can either push or pull an object. If a person pushes a desk across the room, the person is applying force to the desk to make it move. When energy must be added to overcome inertia and gravity, it is applied through muscle or machine.

Normal force is the support force exerted upon an object in contact with another object. The contact between the two objects must be perpendicular—a lamp on a table, for instance, or a book on a shelf. If one object is resting on a surface, the surface is exerting an equal force against the object in order to support the object's weight.

Spring force is the force exerted by a compressed or stretched spring upon any object that is attached to it. An object that compresses or stretches a spring is always acted upon by a force that restores the object to the rest, or equilibrium, position. For most springs, the magnitude of the force is directly proportional to the amount of stretch or compression.

Tension is an oppositional force, that is, it is created when forces act at opposition to each other. For example, when a wire is pulled tight, tension is transmitted through it because forces act from each end. The tensional force is directed along the wire and pulls equally on the objects on either end of the wire.

Objects that are being pulled or pushed may create a dynamic system, one that produces change. Energy is always present in a dynamic system. Energy is a scalar quantity; force is a vector quantity. Forces may be opposed or unopposed. An opposing force will counteract another force. For instance, the force of a rocket taking off can counteract the force of gravity.

We don't live in a closed system, so many forces work on objects—and often work together.

Spring force ensures the safety of bungee jumpers.

Jets face normal, applied, and gravitational
force as well as friction.

FIVE

Picturing Motion

The fact that so many forces work simultaneously on an object can create difficulty for people trying to understand them. Using language to describe the motion of bodies, as well as the forces acting on them, can make the explanations even more complex than usual. Often, charts and diagrams are more effective methods for describing the mathematics behind mechanics, and people find that style of presentation easier to understand.

Free-body diagrams are a form of mathematical language. They are used to show the relative magnitude and direction of all forces acting upon an object in a given situation.

To make a free-body diagram, first choose an object that is subject to motion. Give this object a shape. In the diagrams on page 42, the object is represented by a square, but it could be a more realistic representation. Then, show all the forces that are acting on this object with arrows. This diagram can then be read.

Take It to the Bank

A free-body diagram can help explain why banking—or tilting the road on a curve—can help keep a car on the road.

The forces on a car on the road are its weight (mass times gravity) and the normal force of the road supporting the car. The normal force is perpendicular to the road surface. By banking the curve, the normal force on a car is no longer vertical. It has a horizontal component, which creates centripetal force that will pull the vehicle toward the inside or the center of the curve.

The acceleration of a race car (velocity squared divided by radius of the turn) through a turn increases the force of gravity in a horizontal direction away from the center of the curve; centrifugal force is measured in g-forces. Drivers can experience nearly 5 g's at 230 miles per hour (370 kmh). Traction, which keeps the car on the road, is proportional to the weight on the tires. On banked turns, some of the gravity force is transferred to the car. The larger the degree of banking, the greater the gravity force on the car. When gravity increases, weight increases—and, therefore, traction increases. This is how cars avoid flying off the road at high speeds.

THIS IDEA WON'T FLY

Keep in mind that not every free-body diagram needs to show all forces. For example, in the case of a statue resting on a pedestal, a free-body diagram (Diagram 1) shows the forces of gravity and normal forces supplied by the structure.

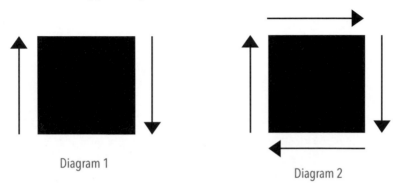

Diagram 1

Diagram 2

Diagram 2 shows four forces acting on an object (the square): normal force, applied force, gravitational force, and friction. The size of the arrow represents the magnitude of the force. In this case, the forces are equal in magnitude. The direction of each arrow reveals the direction in which the force is acting.

Let's say the object in question is an airplane. The gravitational force pulls the plane down, while lift provided by the wings supplies the normal, or supporting, force. Air resistance provides friction, and the jet engines create the applied force. In this case, the applied force must be able to overcome air resistance to such a point that the speed of the plane creates enough lift to overcome the force of gravity. However, if the magnitude of the applied force and the friction are equal, the gravitational force will be greater than the normal force—and there will be a crash.

Engineers and physicists use these diagrams to analyze the forces acting on a body. Using this information, they can design machines that work, such as a plane that can fly.

GLOSSARY

acceleration A change in the velocity of an object.

dynamics The branch of mechanics concerned with the motion of bodies under the action of forces.

force A physical influence that moves something.

friction The force exerted by a surface as an object moves or attempts to move across it.

inertia Resistance to change; the tendency of a body to remain motionless or in motion without acceleration.

kinematics The branch of mechanics concerned with the motion of objects without reference to the forces that cause that action.

linear motion Movement of an object in a straight line.

magnitude The total size of an effect; in a vector it is a number indicating its length.

mass Measure of an object's inertia, the amount of matter that it contains, and its influence in a gravitation field.

GLOSSARY

momentum The measure of movement; the resistance of an object to slowing down.

normal force The support force exerted upon an object that is in contact with another stable object.

scalar A quantity with magnitude but not direction.

speed A measure of how fast an object is moving with regard to time.

tension The force transmitted through a string, cable, or wire when pulled tight at each end.

trajectory The path a projectile makes through space.

uniform motion Motion with no acceleration occurring when forces on an object are balanced.

vector A quantity with magnitude and direction.

velocity The rate at which an object changes its position in a specific direction.

FURTHER INFORMATION

BOOKS

Adair, Robert K. *The Physics of Baseball, Third Edition*. New York, NY: Perennial, 2000.

Allain, Rhett. *Angry Birds Furious Forces: The Physics at Play in the World's Most Popular Game*. Des Moines, IA: National Geographic, 2013.

Bloomfield. Louis A. *How Things Work: The Physics of Everyday Life*. New York, NY: John Wiley & Sons, 1991.

WEBSITES

Institute of Physics
www.physics.org
This site provides videos, news, experiments, and databases that can satisfy the curious mind.

National Aeronautics and Space Administration
www.nasa.gov
Videos, interactive features, and podcasts provide information on what the National Aeronautics and Space Administration is doing.

The Physics Classroom
www.physicsclassroom.com
This comprehensive tutorial provides instruction for beginning physics students, and is an outstanding resource for their teachers.

BIBLIOGRAPHY

Adair, Robert K. *The Physics of Baseball, Third Edition*. New York, NY: Perennial, 2000.

Bloomfield, Louis A. *How Things Work: The Physics of Everyday Life*. New York, NY: John Wiley & Sons, 1991.

Gardner, Robert. *Science Projects About the Physics of Sports*. Berkeley Heights, NJ: Enslow Publishing, 2000.

"How Do You Calculate G-forces?" *HowStuffWorks*. Accessed May 8, 2014. science.howstuffworks.com/science-vs-myth/everyday-myths/question633.htm.

Lopez, Carl, and Danny Sullivan. *Going Faster! Mastering the Art of Race Driving*. Cambridge, MA: Bentley Publishers, 2003.

McPherson, Joyce. *Ocean of Truth: The Story of Sir Isaac Newton*. Lebanon, TN: Greenleaf Press, 1997.

Tyson, Peter. "All About G Forces: What's behind gravity forces, and how much of them can we take?" *NOVA*. November 1, 2007. www.pbs.org/wgbh/nova/space/gravity-forces.html.

INDEX

Page numbers in **boldface** are illustrations.

INDEX